A Note to Parents and Teachers

Dorling Kindersley Readers is a compelling reading programme for beginning readers, designed in conjunction with leading literacy experts, including Cliff Moon, M.Ed., Honorary Fellow of the University of Reading. Cliff Moon has spent many years as a teacher and teacher educator specialising in reading and has written more than 140 books for children and teachers. He reviews regularly for teachers' journals.

Beautiful illustrations and superb full-colour photographs combine with engaging, easy-to-read stories to offer a fresh approach to each subject in the series. Each DK READER is guaranteed to capture a child's interest while developing his or her reading skills, general knowledge and love of reading.

The five levels of DK READERS are aimed at different reading abilities, enabling you to choose the books that are exactly right for your child:

Pre-level 1 – Learning to read
Level 1 – Beginning to read
Level 2 – Beginning to read alone
Level 3 – Reading alone
Level 4 – Proficient readers

The "normal" age at which a child begins to read can be anywhere from three to eight years old, so these levels are intended only as a general guideline.

No matter which level you select, you can be sure that you are helping your child learn to read, then read to learn!

LONDON, NEW YORK, MUNICH,
MELBOURNE, AND DELHI

For DK

Senior Art Editor Rob Perry
Project Manager Sarah Harland
Publishing Manager Julie Ferris
Publishing Manager Simon Beecroft
DTP Designer Lauren Egan
Production Rochelle Talary

Created by Tall Tree Ltd.

Editor Kate Simkins
Designer Ed Simkins

Reading Consultant
Cliff Moon. M.Ed.

This edition published in 2014
First published in Great Britain in 2006 by
Dorling Kindersley Limited,
80 Strand, London WC2R 0RL
A Penguin Random House Company

10 9 8 7 6 5 4 3
003-277244-Sept/14

A catalogue record for this book is available from
the British Library.

Printed and bound in China

ISBN 978-1-4053-1407-7

marvel.com
© 2014 MARVEL

Discover more at
www.dk.com

DK READERS

READING
2
ALONE

MARVEL
SPIDER-MAN
Worst Enemies

Written by Catherine Saunders

Spider-Man is really
a boy called
Peter Parker.
He uses his special
powers to help
people, but he has many enemies.
One of them is Norman Osborn,
who calls himself the Green Goblin.
He got his powers when
some chemicals exploded.

Goblin vehicle
The Green Goblin
flies around on
a Goblin Glider.
He has invented
a special gas to put
people to sleep!

The Green Goblin's greatest wish
is to kill Spider-Man.
But Spider-Man is stronger and
faster than his enemy.

The Hobgoblin,
another enemy of Spider-Man,
found the chemicals that gave
the Green Goblin his powers.
He used them to make himself strong.

No one knows who
the Hobgoblin
really is.

All he wants is to be rich, and
he will fight anyone who tries
to stop him, even Spider-Man.

Goblin grenades
The Hobgoblin's weapons
include Jack O'Lanterns,
goblin grenades and
sharp throwing bats.
He flies a bat-glider.

Otto Octavius is a brilliant scientist.
He had a freak accident during
an experiment with robot arms.
The robot arms stuck to him.
He became the evil Doctor Octopus
and Spider-Man's enemy.

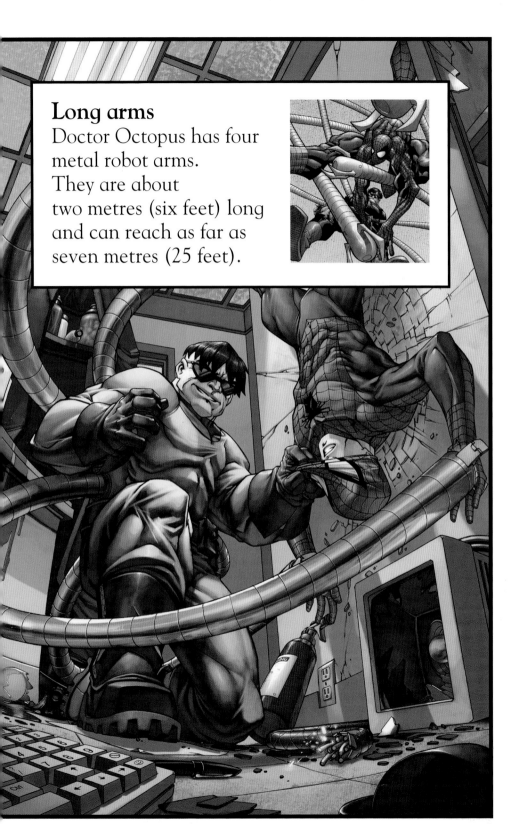

Long arms

Doctor Octopus has four
metal robot arms.
They are about
two metres (six feet) long
and can reach as far as
seven metres (25 feet).

The Scorpion is twice as strong as Spider-Man, and he is also quicker. The Scorpion is really a private detective called Mac Gargan.

The Scorpion's tail is as tall as
a man and can fire powerful blasts
at his enemies.
Spider-Man cannot beat
the Scorpion in a fight
so he must out-think him.

Rhino is one of Spider-Man's
most powerful enemies.
Underneath his bulletproof suit,
he is really a man called Alex O'Hirn.

Strong and fast
When he charges,
Rhino can reach
a top speed of nearly
160 kilometres
(100 miles) per hour.

Rhino is incredibly strong and
feels almost no pain.
He can crush cars, trucks and even
buildings, but he really wants
to crush Spider-Man!

Venom is part human, part alien.
The human part is Eddie Brock,
a man who hates Spider-Man.
The alien part can disguise himself
as anything.

Venom is the only
creature that
Spider-Man's spider-
sense cannot detect.
This makes him one
of Spider-Man's most
dangerous enemies.

The Vulture steals from rich people because he wants wealth and power. He is really an inventor called Adrian Toomes, who created a special harness to make himself fly.

Peter Parker worked out how to stop the Vulture from flying. Spider-Man could then defeat his enemy.

The Lizard is really Doctor Connors, who lost an arm while in the army. He studied reptiles to try and learn from them how to grow a new arm. His experiment went badly wrong and turned Connors into the Lizard.

The Lizard's aim is to rid the world of humans and that makes him Spider-Man's enemy!

A lightning strike turned
Max Dillon into Electro,
one of Spider-Man's
most dangerous enemies.

Electro can control electricity.
He uses it to travel through
the air and
to give himself
extra strength.

Electric weapon
Electro uses blasts of
electricity as weapons.
He can fire them
up to 30 metres
(100 feet).

Quentin Beck dreamt of being
a film star, but he didn't have
the looks or talent.
He learnt special effects and stunts
and decided to use these skills to
become a Super Hero instead.

Clever boots
Mysterio has special boots that release smoke. They also have springs to help him make huge leaps.

He turned into Mysterio and tried to become famous by capturing Spider-Man. But Mysterio failed, and he wants revenge!

Most people know that Spider-Man
is a good guy.
But some people think
he is bad news.
Professor Spencer Smythe
believes that
Spider-Man is trouble.

He invented robots
called Spider-Slayers to
destroy Spider-Man.

But Spider-Man was much smarter than the robots and beat them easily.

The Sandman is a clever enemy.
He can turn his body into sand and
become any shape.

Hydro-Man blames
Spider-Man for
the accident that
made him able to
turn into water.

One day,
Hydro-Man and
the Sandman
helped each other
to fight Spider-Man.
But a freak accident made them
join together and turn into
a giant mud creature.
Spider-Man easily defeated
the monster.

Kraven is from
Russia, but
he ran away
from home when
he was a child.

He is a clever
hunter who can
find any animal.

When a witch doctor's potion
increased Kraven's power,
he decided to hunt Spider-Man.

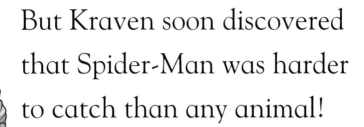

But Kraven soon discovered that Spider-Man was harder to catch than any animal!

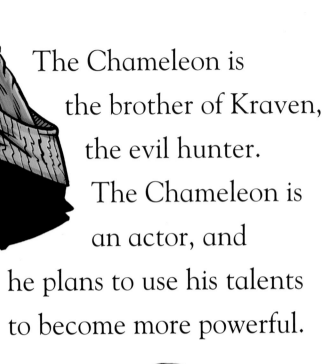

The Chameleon is the brother of Kraven, the evil hunter. The Chameleon is an actor, and he plans to use his talents to become more powerful.

Mask master
The Chameleon can make life-like masks, but his tricks and disguises do not fool Spider-Man!

Spider-Man knows
that he must stop the Chameleon.
Anyone who hurts people or breaks
the law is Spider-Man's enemy.
As long as Spider-Man is around,
his enemies will never win!

Fascinating Facts

Peter Parker's parents were killed when he was a baby. He lived with his Uncle Ben and Aunt May.

When he was a student, Peter became Spider-Man after he was bitten by a spider.

Peter Parker wears his Spider-Man costume under his clothes.

Peter is good at science. He invented Spider-Man's web and web shooters.

Spider-Man can sense danger thanks to his spider-sense.